Path to the Light

God is Light

Now the message that we have heard from his Son and announce is this: God is light, and there is no darkness at all in him (GNT)

1 John 1:5

Path to the Light

Your Journey out of Darkness

STEVEN MCLEMORE

This is a work of fiction. The events and characters described herein are imaginary and are not intended to refer to specific places or living persons. The opinions expressed in this manuscript are solely the opinions of the author and do not represent the opinions or thoughts of the publisher. The author has represented and warranted full ownership and/or legal right to publish all the materials in this book.

Path to the Light
Your Journey out of Darkness
All Rights Reserved.
Copyright © 2016 Steven McLemore
v5.0

Cover Design © 2016 Cover Ed Davis. Illustrations by Dennis Winston. All rights reserved - used with permission.

All Biblical references unless otherwise noted, were taken from the following sources:
King James Version (KJV) copyright ©
New International Version (NIV) copyright ©
Good News Translations (GNT) copyright ©

This book may not be reproduced, transmitted, or stored in whole or in part by any means, including graphic, electronic, or mechanical without the express written consent of the publisher except in the case of brief quotations embodied in critical articles and reviews.

MOSA Publishing
P.O. Box 3306
Henrico, VA 23228

ISBN: 978-0-9910208-0-5

Library of Congress Control Number: 2015921317

PRINTED IN THE UNITED STATES OF AMERICA

Dedication

First and foremost, I give thanks to Almighty God, our Creator, for choosing me to write such an important and necessary book.

God inspired me by giving me the will, knowledge, and determination to write. Likewise, He provided me the resources to see this book through to completion. I am truly grateful, honored, and blessed with this opportunity to do God's will.

- My daughters, Sabrina and Monica; my sisters, Ernestine and Teresa—who believed in and encouraged me.

- The relatives and friends who said a prayer on my behalf that my eyes be opened to the powerful, unchanging Word of God.

Table of Contents

Dedication v
Acknowledgments xi
Foreword xiii
Introduction xv
    Understanding Interpretation and Translations xvii
    How to Understand and Use This Book: xix

Chapter I - ABOUT THE BIBLE 1
    Path to the Light 2
    The Divine Library 4
    Bible Translations 6
    Why the Bible 8
    Missing the Word 11
    In Context 12

Chapter II - LESSONS FROM THE SCRIPTURES 15
    Noah's Ark (Cleanse the Earth) 17
    Heavenly Rewards (Crowns) 18
    Save Me (Salvation) 20
    Let It Go (Forgiveness) 22
    False Teachers (Deceivers) 24

Chapter III - ALMIGHTY GOD 27
    Our Invisible God 28
    Essence of Life 30
    In God's Time 32
    God's Oldest Twins 34
    What God Hates 36

Chapter IV - JESUS CHRIST 39
- A Christmas Present 40
- King of Kings 42
- He Showed Us How 44
- The Last Supper 46
- Man's Darkest Day/(The Resurrection) 48
- Gave You My All 50

Chapter V - THE (HOLY) SPIRIT 53
- The Helper 54
- Don't Lie to Me 56
- Spiritual Fruit 58
- Spiritually Connected 60
- Spiritual Warfare 62
- Prepare for Battle 64

Chapter VI - PRAYER 67
- Heavenly Bound 68
- My Secret Place 70
- Special Bread 71
- Prayer Menu 72
- Just Ask 74
- Answering Prayers 76

Chapter VII - CHRISTIAN FAITH 79
- Faith Believers 80
- Christian Doctrine 82
- Christian Walk 84
- The Struggle 86
- When God Calls You 88
- More Than a Sermon 90

Chapter VIII - ANGELS & DEMONS 93
- Spiritual Messengers 94
- Angel Talk 96
- In the Den 98
- Beware of Evil 100
- The Final Judgment 103

Chapter IX - WISDOM 105
    Our Greatest Fear 107
    Our Life, God's Plan.. 108
    Listen to the Lord 110
    Free Will... 112
    True Peace.. 114
    A Great Secret 116
    Spiritual Delight.. 118

Conclusion.. 120

Glossary 122

Index 125

Appendix A - The 66 Books of The Bible 134

Appendix B - The Old Testament Bible Verses
              In Chronological Order 135

Appendix C - The New Testament Bible Verses
              In Chronological Order 136

Acknowledgments

I want to personally and sincerely thank Reverend Michelle Hatcher for her invaluable assistance, her Biblical knowledge, and spiritual wisdom. She provided guidance in helping me stay focused on the correct path and task God has laid out for me.

The unique gifts and talents of my good friends, Deborah Johnson, Helen Harris, Danielle Greene, and my niece Joy McMillian, who helped see the potential of this book.

Finally, my pastor, Dr. Kirkland R. Walton of St. Peter Baptist church, Glen Allen, VA, provided spiritual leadership. His diligence and devotion makes him a true follower of God and His Word.

Foreword

This journey we call life is filled with twists and turns. Even with all that has been invented, the GPS, worldwide web, and social media, there are still questions that human invention *cannot* answer. There is a continuous daily search for comfort, strength, purpose, and understanding. In *Path to the Light*, the reader is encouraged to follow the path to the ultimate Light for direction and guidance with their choices on the road of life.

The author, Steven McLemore, believes that the Light is God and the pathway is God's Word. Steve is constantly listening to God for insightful ways to share the Gospel. His devotion to God, enthusiasm, and zeal for life motivate him to spin the struggles and delights of life into poetry. He has written poetry for many years, and excitedly approached me about compiling this collection of poems about five years ago. His love for the Bible has led him to write these poems with the purpose of creating stepping stones that can help lead the reader to the Word of God. In these poems, he shares his beliefs about various aspects of Christian life: our relationships with God, Jesus, and The Holy Spirit, as well as our service in the church, our personal walk, etc.

Steve hopes that his poetry will make readers think about various topics, and inspire the desire to dig deeper into the Bible and seek God for greater understanding. Biblical references, a glossary, and an index are provided to encourage the reader to study. Each poem conveys the specific intent to assist the reader in recognizing that there is *hope, healing, and help* for the situations we face in our daily lives.

In the poem "Our Life, God's Plan," Steve enthusiastically offers a glimpse of God's design and shows the simplicity of our relationship with God. "Heavenly Bound," a peek at the promise, is there to encourage hearts and prompt us to remain faithful. "A Christmas Present" takes us to an old story with an eternal lesson: the true gift of Christmas is Love. As I read "When God Calls You," I was reminded of the responsibility given to us and our commitment to God. While "Let It Go" gives readers the tools to aid in their healing when wronged—this poem offers the knowledge and power of forgiveness in life; it also shares the dangers of holding on to grudges and offenses.

I hope all who read this collection are moved to strengthen their relationship with God. It is truly Steve's sincere desire to inspire anyone in need; whether one is looking for a daily devotion, an occasional reminder, or seeking to begin a personal relationship with our Creator, These poems were written to provide a *Path to the Light*.

Reverend Michelle E. Hatcher

Samuel DeWitt Proctor

School of Theology

at Virginia Union University

Introduction

We hear people say they want to go to Heaven when they die.

Well, we are all going to die, but we all ain't going to Heaven.

Our life's journey is taking us somewhere.

What path are *you* on? Where are *you* going?

Who are *you* following?

Like many people today, I enjoy traveling, going places I have never been and experiencing new adventures. While en route, I often need the assistance of a map. However, I must have some knowledge of how to use such items as its key scale, orientation, lines, and colored notations. If we apply this same principle in our journey through life, we can greatly improve the quality of our lives. The Bible, the Word of God, is the best instructional map for us to achieve the quality of life that we so often seek.

Taking full advantage of what the Bible has to offer is incredibly wise. First, there are some important facts that we must know. This book of poems, *Path to the Light*, is designed to empower you by answering some fundamental biblical questions you may have been pondering. Think of this book as a bridge to the Holy Bible that has as its mission to relay educational information about the Bible. From the curious to new believers and seasoned Christians alike, there is something in this book for everyone.

If you are one who desires to increase your knowledge, wisdom, and understanding of life, then you will come to realize how valuable this book is. You will learn important facts, such as what the Bible truly is, how the Bible was compiled, why there are different Bible translations, the Godhead (the Trinity), the different types of prayers, Scriptural lessons, what Christians believe, and much much more. After reading these poems, you will be better equipped to approach the Bible with understanding and meaning of what the Bible is and how the Bible can impact your life.

Path to the Light will take you on a journey to 36 different books and more than 200 verses in the Bible. These poems are enlightening, uplifting, and inspiring. You will begin to feel more confident in your spiritual walk as your knowledge of God's Word grows. You will gain a greater appreciation for why the Bible was written and why God intended His Word to be the *center of our lives*. God's Word is given to us so that we may learn to live according to His will. *"To God Be the Glory!"* Various poems will lead you to thought-provoking, possibly soul-searching moments. These poems can also be used as a teaching tool or topic for discussion during Bible study class or home study.

God wants us to live in His marvelous Light and enjoy life, yet be aware of the dangers associated with darkness. You will learn what happened to some who were deceived and chose to journey down a path of darkness. As you travel through your life's journey, you may encounter, at times, darkness along the way. It is there to deceive you, but *you do have help*.

Light is all you need to guide and keep you moving in the right direction. Light does not hide things; Light reveals the truth of what is. This is why Light in your life is so essential. You need only one Light and one set of directions for your eternal life. When you follow the right directions for life, *The Bible*, and are guided by the right Light, *God*, then your life's journey will take you to the eternal and right place, *Heaven*, in the end.

**This book is not attempting to replace the Bible.
That is an impossible and unrealistic task!**

I <u>hearten</u> you to please read with an open mind.

Understanding Interpretation and Translations

When people describe an object, they may use different words in their interpretation of the object. For example, one person may say it is "big," another that it is "large," and still another that it is "huge." What we know for certain about this object—it is not small and it has some size to it. The focus here is on the common interpretation of the words.

A foreign language translator needs a thorough knowledge and understanding of the people, their language, customs, culture, and most importantly, the time period of the writing being translated. All are crucial factors. Different translators may use different words to describe the same thing, based on those factors and their own life experiences, knowledge, and backgrounds. Keep in mind that *the meaning of the words*, and not the word itself, is significant. Since different languages use different words, there may not be an equivalent word for the translation. Translators understand this; thus, they focus on *the meaning of words*. **(The translation process is not perfect.)**

Today, there are many different Bible translations. In this book, *Path to the Light*, the poem "Bible Translations" addresses this concern. I believe Biblical scholars did not see this translation process as a major problem, as long as the focus remained on *the meaning of the words*.

For the purposes of this book, three translations of the Bible are used. They are: the King James Version (KJV), New International Version (NIV), and the Good News Translation (GNT).

As you search in your Bible for the verses mentioned in this book, you may notice a difference in the wording. This is due to the different Bible translations that were used. Please keep in mind that *the meaning of the words* that is significant.

Comparison chart explaining the different types of Bibles

King James Vision (KJV)	New International Version (NIV)	Good News Translations (GNT)
† An old English translation † Completed in 1611, commissioned by King James I of England and is a very well-known Bible today. † It is Written in the old English dialect, the way in which people spoke in England at that time and place in history. † This Bible is written in a type known as *"word-for-word."*	† One of the newer English translations † Completed in 1978, published by Biblica formally known as The International Bible Society † It is written in the American modern English dialect we speak today; this allows us to gain a better understanding of what the Bible is trying to tell us. † This Bible is a blend between *"word-for-word"* and *"thought-for-thought."*	† One of the newer English translations † Completed in 1976, published by the American Bible Society it was formally known as The Today's English Version (TEV) † It is written in the American modern English dialect we speak today; this allows us to gain a better understanding of what the Bible is trying to tell us. † This Bible is written in a type known as *"thought-for-thought."*

How to Understand and Use This Book:

This book is more than just poetry; it will put you on the path to changing your life for the better.

Picture yourself standing at the edge of a bridge. There is a powerful Light source on the other side of the bridge attracting your attention. Curiosity captivates you, so you decide to go and investigate this Light. With every step you take on this path toward the Light, you feel the connection growing stronger between you and the Light. The closer you get to the Light, the more truth about life is revealed. You begin to see the world differently. Your knowledge, wisdom, and understanding increase as you continue traveling forward on this *Path to the Light*.

Consider:

> Each poem: a step closer to the Light,
>
> Each Bible verse: God's Word revealed to you,
>
> The Light: God

"it" underlined in this book is referring to evil

Your Journey awaits you—are you ready?

"We can easily forgive a child who is afraid of the dark;
the real tragedy of life is when men are afraid
of the Light."

Plato 427-347 BC

Chapter I

About the BIBLE

"The best evidence of the *Bible* being
the Word of God is found between the covers."

Charles Hodge 1797-1878

Path to the Light

John 1:1-5

Life is an unknown journey
from the moment our lives began
It is important to know which way to go
to succeed we must have a plan

Our thoughts develop direction
direction puts us on a path [1]
But keep in mind before you *choose*
you will encounter some aftermath

On one path we're guided by Light [2]
to help us along our way
Other paths lead into the dark
but the dark can lead us astray

We should never consider a path in the dark
we will stumble because we can't see [3]
The dark will gain control over us
<u>it</u> will cause us much misery

The dark can never reveal the truth
in there truth does not exist
The dark you must know *hates* the Light
but us, <u>it</u> will never dismiss

The Light is our source of power
equipped to give our life spark
Always stay focused on the Light
because wickedness thrives in the dark

God is the Light we need in our lives
come travel this path and see
God's Word, the Bible, is the right path
if we long for our true destiny

As we move to the Light we will learn the truth
how to live and keep our path clear [4]
Our knowledge and understanding will grow
as we learn we have nothing to fear

The beauty of traveling in the Light
is to know we are never alone
Here we connect with the ultimate power
God who sits high on His throne.

[1] Psalms 16:11   [2] John 8:12   [3] Proverbs 4:19
[4] Ephesians 5:8-11

The Divine Library
Mark 13:31

There was a special library built
a very long time ago
This took about 1500 years
to complete for all to know

We are told about 40 writers were picked
who listened and followed God's plan [1]
To tell the story of life on earth
from creation then later to man

They lived on different continents
and had different writing techniques
From Africa, Asia, and Europe
speaking Hebrew, Aramaic, and Greek

They wrote and told about the past
the present, and future times
History, prophecy, gospels, the law
see this is what they were assigned

The people they wrote stories about
and the changes they underwent
The dreams, the storms, the walks of faith
and even cruel punishment

Now some of these writers were chosen
to write of a special Son [2]
Who told and showed us how we are to live;
you see He was the Chosen One

This library has two major parts
the Old and New Testaments
The Old, the foundation of life as we know
the New, Jesus and His life's intent

You too can see this library today
if you are willing to open and look
This library *is* God's Holy Bible
all for you within Sixty-Six Books.

[1] Romans 15:4   [2] 1 John 5:10-12

THE BIBLE IS A LIBRARY

(Complete listing of Bible books on page 134)

Bible Translations

2 Peter 1:20-21

You go to purchase a Holy Bible
but which are you going to choose
With all the different Bibles today
you can't help but be somewhat confused

Why so many Bible translations
when we say there is only one God
Translating from Hebrew, Aramaic, and Greek
to English at times can be odd

Translation is taking a foreign language
which is unfamiliar to you
And have it interpreted into your language
so you will be able to use

Interpreting language is no easy task
and the process can be very slow
Learn other cultures, what their words mean
translators must study to know

So Bible scholars have settled on
two main different philosophies
To translate the Bible word-for-word
or is thought where the focus should be

Some scholars chose to write word-for-word (KJV)
matching words as close as they can
As they tried to maintain sentence structure
feeling this was a better plan

Some scholars chose to write thought-for-thought (GNT)
they believed this method works best
The importance here is not matching words
but the original thought of the text

The more you read the Word of God
and learn what God has to say
You may want to read both word and thought
some comprehend better this way

Some Bible translations address this need
with word and thought they have both (NIV)
Providing us with a blended view
to assist with your spiritual growth

In time you may move to a Study Bible
as you seriously seek to learn more
The scholarly notes help to explain
the Scriptures when you are unsure

But always beware of the Bible you read
and the message that Bible contains
Other religions use Bibles too
but their messages are not the same [1]

As you're looking to purchase a Holy Bible
to learn God's Word and His plan
Which Bible translation is best you may ask
the Bible you best understand.

[1] Revelation 22:18-19

Why the Bible
2 Timothy 3:16

If a better life is what you seek
then no longer will you have to look
The Holy Bible is waiting for you
this is your life instructional book

Why, because this is God's Word
there is no better place you can go
To gain insight to your better life
God's concerned with your life as you grow

The beginning of knowledge is fear of the Lord [1]
now this is the best place to start
When you trust in God, and live by His Word
from you God will never depart

Here you will learn of the Trinity
how the Godhead is three in one
God the Father, the Holy Spirit
and Jesus, God's begotten Son

Wisdom will come into your life
as you strive to grow spiritually
God will know your faith is real
when you learn to wait patiently

You will learn why you are *not* to complain [2]
when things do not go your way
And if someone chooses to do you wrong
you will learn why for them you're to pray

You will learn the wise way to communicate
with your ears and then with your mouth
Be quick to listen and slow to speak ³
whenever you have thoughts of doubt

Learn how you're blessed with the gift of free will
the power God gives you to choose
But consequences are sure to arise
whenever this power is misused

In time you will learn the true meaning of peace
the only way peace is achieved
Is when your life is in union with Christ
then God knows what you truly believe

And as your transformation takes place
you will learn about spiritual fruit
This gift from God will improve your life
in ways you can never dispute

You will learn why you are told to forgive
Jesus said this is what we must do
Think of some things you've done in your life
aren't you glad God's forgiven you?

You will also learn of salvation
the eternal gift of this word
How we can be saved from this sinful world
regardless of what you have heard

You will learn why you're *never* satisfied [4]
why greed keeps infecting your mind
Your desire for more grows out of control
disobeying God's Word at times

In time you will learn to identify
false teachers as they appear
Not to be moved by their misleading words
they so desperately want you to hear

You will learn to beware of the evil one
its purpose and why it exists
Why you must put on the whole armor of God
your protection to help you resist

We can look to science for physical proof
when unbelievers try to attack
Anthropologists and archeologists
have unearthed many historical facts [5]

This and much more can better your life
in ways like you never knew
If a better life is your true desire
than the Bible is waiting on you.

[1] Proverbs 1:7   [2] Philippians 2:14-15   [3] James 1:19
[4] Proverbs 27:20   [5] Google this

Missing the Word

Luke 6:46

We grab our Bible on Sunday morning
and it's off to church we go
To spend some time in fellowship [1]
with believers to spiritually grow

The congregation gets settled in
as the preacher delivers God's Word
Then we leave church feeling really good
from the sermon we willingly heard

The Bible is the Word of God
filled with moral lessons for us [2]
But our problem is for the rest of the week
God's Word we don't live or discuss

We are just too busy with other things
that won't bring us closer to Him
These are known as worldly things
which more often will lead us to sin

The only way we will stay ahead
and make sure we are not left behind
Is every day spend time in God's Word
to nurture our spiritual minds

A week has passed, it's Sunday again
so it's back to church we will go
Again we attend with Bible in hand
is yours to read or is yours for show?

[1] 1 John 1:7   [2] Luke 11:28

In Context

2 Timothy 3:15

The Bible is the Word of God
written for us to read
To help us learn what God has to say
and connect with Him spiritually

Some like to read and quote a verse
then tell you what that verse means
But when verses are taken out of context
the damage can be quite extreme

When taking a verse out of context
we are not learning the Word as God planned
This surely can lead to wrong conclusions
and can lead us to misunderstand

Context is what completes the verse
what is written above and below
All has to be read to learn what God said
if the truth we desire to know

Context is truly the focal point
it's important to stay on God's track
What is being said, the grammar used,
synthesis, and historical facts

All these components are necessary,
when learning God's Word His way
If we don't understand how important this is
others will lead us astray

How can we be sure if one's words are of God?
this question may enter your mind
If we have obeyed and studied God's Word [1]
we can tell if one's words are divine

Each time God's Word is shared with us
the thing we should always think next
Is what we're being told, how God's Word is used,
and are they used in their proper context.

[1] 2 Timothy 2:15

Chapter II

Lessons from the SCRIPTURES

"Nobody ever outgrows *Scriptures*;
the book widens and deepens with our years."

Charles Spurgeon 1834 –1892

Noah's Ark

Genesis 6:8-22, 7, 8, 9:1-16

Long ago God got upset
with the evil His people displayed
So God called Noah, a righteous man
who listened to what God had to say

*"Make yourself an Ark out of wood
three hundred cubits long,
fifty cubits wide, thirty cubits high"*
for this cargo it must be built strong

Noah was told to put in the Ark
his wife, his sons, and their wives
And to collect a pair of each animal
so all species were sure to survive

Then God made it rain forty days and nights
and the water began to rise
This flood was to cleanse the earth of man's sin
God's wrath caught them all by surprise

On the forty-first day the rain did end
and a dove flew in search of dry land
Returning in time with an olive branch
that was placed into Noah's hand

God promised Noah there'd be no more floods
and the spectacular way God shows
After it rains as the sun starts to shine
God's Word is confirmed by His rainbow.

Heavenly Rewards

Proverbs 11:18

Our works alone will not get us to Heaven
salvation is the only way
And some who arrive will get their reward
if they have followed God's Word and obeyed

These rewards are known as crowns
the receivers will be very few
Only given to those who truly believe
and did what God said we are to do

We start with *the incorruptible crown*
keep your bodies in shape for the race [1]
So in the end you will win the prize
when your loyalty has proven your case

The crown of rejoicing is for those who lead
unbelievers to Jesus Christ [2]
And get them prepared for His return
this is our hope, our joy, and advice

There is also *the crown of righteousness*
this is known as the victory prize [3]
For keeping the faith to finish the course
our commitment shows God we are wise

The crown of life is a costly one
your endurance is put to the test [4]
Stay faithful and suffer for Jesus Christ
fight temptation and you will be blessed

The crown of glory is for those who teach
feed the flock God's Word so they'll hear [5]
Serve the Lord, explain His will
stay humble, stay strong, and sincere

Salvation assures us a place in Heaven
there no one is wearing a frown
But for true believers who live to please God
God awaits them to give them their crown.

[1] 1 Corinthians 9:25   [2] 1 Thessalonians 2:19
[3] 2 Timothy 4:8   [4] James 1:12   [5] 1 Peter 5:4

Save Me

Acts 16:30-31

The serpent deceived Eve and said,
"You will not certainly die" [1]
"For God knows when you eat of this fruit
like Him it will open your eyes"

This is the day sin entered our world
from the moment they took their first bite
Evil convinced them to disobey God
as it steered them away from the Light

Today the world is infested with sin
as we do what God said not to do
Sin keeps us separated from God
God's Word lets us know this is true [2]

God loves us so and He always knows
the evil promoting our sin
He provided the way for us to be saved
through salvation, that's how we begin [3]

God sent His Son, Jesus, down to earth [4]
He told how salvation is achieved
All we have to do is confess, have faith
and live as we truly believe

We become saved through Jesus Christ
He alone can free us from sin
Salvation is the path to God
but first you must be born again

Salvation protects us from God's wrath [5]
it's our spiritual deliverance
God's grace makes this clear—it's not based on works [6]
salvation is free and does not cost a cent

The day we repent and turn to God
our sins will be wiped away [7]
Then we can enjoy a new way of life
unconcerned by what others may say

Not everyone will make this wise choice
because many do not understand
Life was designed for God's purpose alone
from the moment God gave life to man.

[1] Genesis 3:1-5   [2] Ephesians 5:6   [3] John 10:9
[4] 1 John 4:9   [5] 1 Thessalonians 5:9   [6] Ephesians 2:8-9
[7] Acts 3:19

Let It Go

Mark 11:25-26

In life when someone does us wrong
it can hurt to the core of our hearts
Especially when it is by someone we love
the pain can tear us apart

This pain can cause anger to rise
then revenge starts to enter our minds
Getting them back is all we think of
but with God we are now out of line

We must keep in mind it is only a test
God told us how we are to win
Follow His Word and do what He says
we should never consider revenge

Now this is the part where we get confused
because many do not understand
Our human nature desires revenge
but God has a much different plan

"Vengeance is mine, sayeth the Lord" [1]
we know God knows what is best
God will handle those who wrong us
so there is no need for us to get stressed

We are to forgive those who have wronged us
like God has forgiven us
We all have come short of the glory of God [2]
this matter we need not discuss

Peter asked Jesus "how many times
with others are we to forgive"
"Seventy times seven" Jesus replied [3]
in other words as long as we live

Forgiveness means we are to forget
we're to learn how to live God's way [4]
What is done is done; move on with our lives
as God said, for them we are to pray

Lack of forgiving can turn into grudge
and can lead to much bitterness
While the one who has caused us the pain
has moved on; they're not getting upset

There are no guarantees in life
hard times God said would be so [5]
When we learn someone has done us wrong
to please God we must just let it go.

[1] Romans 12:19   [2] Romans 3:23   [3] Matthew 18:21-22
[4] Colossians 3:13   [5] Isaiah 30:20

False Teachers

2 Peter 2:1-3

This is a very important poem
please take this one seriously
If we do not, we may find ourselves
in a place we do not wish to be

It is important to study God's Word
to learn and understand
The truth of how God wants us to live
according to life as He planned

Biblical teachers are here to teach
God's Word of how we are to live
Their focus should be on God and His plan
and never their personal motives

The Bible warns false teachers will rise
false Prophets and Christians as well [1]
It is up to us to know God's Word
so false teachers we are able to tell

They lost their way a long time ago
when their minds became focused on greed
They let evil in to rule their hearts
evil has no apologies

Their corrupted minds and counterfeit faith
will keep those who don't know amused [2]
But in the end they are going to pay
for the Scriptures they *choose* to misuse

False teachers are much like vicious wolves [3]
on the prowl to devour our souls
They will tell us lies, make them sound like the truth
to disguise their deceiving roles [4]

False teachers will tell us anything
and will show us they have the proof
But when compared to Scripture context
we will see how they're twisting the truth [5]

The Bible foretells a time will come
when sound doctrines some don't want to hear
Folks' only concerns are their greedy desires
and to please their own itching ears [6]

Are they telling the truth about Jesus Christ
how He died, was buried, then rose
Do they say God said, *"This is My Son"*
or this do they simply oppose?

Is their teaching in line with the Gospel,
do they teach of the Trinity?
Do you *feel* their words glorifying God
is their focus where it needs to be?

If we do not read and study God's Word
the truth we will never know
False teachers will have us believing in them
and with them to Hell we will go.

[1] Mark 13:22-23 [2] 2 Corinthians 11:13 [3] Matthew 7:15
[4] Colossians 2:8 [5] Romans 16:17-18 [6] 2 Timothy 4:3-4

Chapter III

Almighty GOD

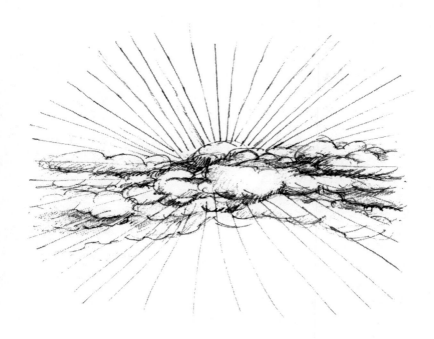

"We are, because *God* is."

Emanuel Swedenborg 1688-1772

Our Invisible God

Romans 1:20

We all can agree we believe what we see
when our eyes are focused on it
But what of the things we cannot see
we are quick to deny or omit

Invisible things we know do exist
like the wind, the movement of air
When an object seems to move by itself
the wind's power is currently there

An invisible power we too possess
and we have it internally
Doctors can check us from head to toe
but this power they will never see

Encased in our head is our brain
a physical mass of cells
Within our brain resides our mind
forming thoughts to help us excel

See the mind is a non-physical force
where all of our thoughts accrue
How the mind works this still is unknown
Doctors know what I'm saying is true

A non-physical force is in control
of our physical brain's routine
Yet the most amazing thing about this is
the mind has never been seen

Our powerful mind cannot be seen
but we often obey its commands
Our invisible God is much the same [1]
God, we will never fully understand

Many know what I say is true
as you are reading and thinking of this
So why is it when there is talk about God
fools are quick to deny God exists? [2]

God we know is non-physical
yet He has given commands to us
I have already proved the unseen is real
now the question, in God will *you* trust?

We are told what we see is temporary
do not focus on man-made things [3]
God has a much grander plan in mind
for all of His human beings

In life we believe what we see
yet God's Word offers so much more
What we see we are told is not going to last
but God's Word lasts forevermore.

[1] 1 Timothy 1:17   [2] Psalms 14:1   [3] 2 Corinthians 4:18

Essence of Life

Matthew 3:16-17

Life, all should know, is a gift from God
without God we could not survive
It is God's will for us to exist
He alone is why we are alive

How can we ever learn all about God?
He is greater than any abyss [1]
God is too vast for our limited minds
so the Bible tells how God exists

The Father, the Son, the Holy Spirit
all three at the same time are God
Christians know this as the Trinity
unbelievers may think this is odd

The Father *created* everything
and all we have come to know [2]
He is omnipresent, knows everything,
and He wants us to spiritually grow

Jesus, the Son, was *fashioned* as man [3]
He came here in human form
He humbly told of the Kingdom of God
but to enter one must first transform

The Holy Spirit *indwells* with all
who have given their life to Christ
He comforts and aids in our spiritual growth
as He gives us true Godly advice [4]

There is much in life we do not understand
because we are human beings
God is much more than we will ever know
and prefers to remain unseen

God alone is the Essence of Life
to Him nothing will ever compare
We cannot understand all God is
but His Word tells us how much He cares

God gives us life and all that is
because He is the great "I AM" [5]
Nothing is more important than God
we must learn how to live by His plan.

[1] Isaiah 55:8-9   [2] Genesis 1, 2   [3] Philippians 2:8
[4] John 14:26   [5] Exodus 3:14

The Trinity Shield

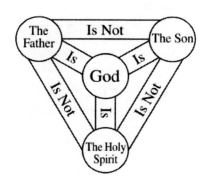

In God's Time
1 Peter 5:6

People will often do what they want
for their pleasure and their own delight
But when problems arise they seem surprised
could it be the time was not right?

When is the right time to do what we want
is this something we can decide?
Or should we look to Almighty God
for His wisdom; His love will provide

The Bible tells us be patient and wait
this surely God wants us to do
He will let us know when it is time
because God will forever be true [1]

We have been told to trust in God
lean not on what we understand
But some do not believe in God's Word
and prefer to live by their plan

So they foolishly go and move before God
they are determined to have things their way
Later to find the timing was wrong
and the outcome is making them pay

But for all who understand God's Word
and wait till God tells them to move
They reap the reward with peace of mind
because patience God loves and virtue

This is a lesson we all need to know
it's important and very unique
Do not make a move until God tells you
pay attention to God when He speaks

If you want to receive a message from God
stay alert; He will give you a sign
Learn His Word, obey Him, and pray
He will tell you to move in His time.

[1] Deuteronomy 7:9

God's Oldest Twins

Hebrews 4:16

God has always been about love
from the very beginning of time
He continues to show He cares for us
we are constantly on His mind

At times He can be pleased with us
until we engage in sin [1]
That's when He knows we do need His help
so He calls His compassionate twins

Each has a unique personality
and their mission they always fulfill
Their special gifts given by God
guarantee they can handle God's will

They are always prepared and ready to serve
anytime, anywhere, anyplace
God alone tells them where they are to go
and their names are Mercy and Grace

Mercy appears when we have done wrong
to protect and keep us preserved [2]
From the consequences we should endure
and the adversity we truly deserve

Grace can appear unannounced
as a blessing unearned from above [3]
When we don't get what we do deserve
God is showing His goodness and love

They have an effect on so many lives
several have undergone change
Some have submitted and come to Christ
now their lives are no longer the same

When you encounter one of these twins
understand at that time you are blessed
This is God showing His favor to you
thank God and to others attest

Now you are aware of Mercy and Grace
the work they are committed to do
Whenever they come into your life
God is showing how much He loves you.

[1] Ecclesiastes 7:20   [2] Titus 3:4-5   [3] John 1:16

What God Hates

Proverbs 6:16-19

God lets us know He cares for us
by the love He continues to give
His infallible Word, the Holy Bible
our instructions on how we are to live

The Bible tells us of many things
about life which we can relate
God also makes this very clear
with this list of the things He hates

A proud look on one is not a good thing
God knows the thoughts on one's mind
Evil desires lead them to do wrong
and to someone they will not be kind

A lying tongue is never good
untrue words to keep us deceived
Misleading people deliberately
hoping their lies are believed

Hands out to shed innocent blood
stay alert and always beware
There is no limit how far they will go
to see us in distress or despair

A heart that devises wicked plans
this person is not in a rush
Insidious thoughts to get what they want
knowing someone will surely get crushed

Feet that are quick to rush into evil
do travel a wicked dark path
Yet time will reveal what they have done
when they're faced with the aftermath

A false witness that speaketh lies
will speak out on what they don't know
Creating stories rooted in lies
with each word it continues to grow

Someone who stirs up trouble with friends
will never bring anyone peace
If you *choose* to stay connected with them
your problems are sure to increase

Now you know these things God hates
because each will lead us to sin
Just keep in mind when you *choose* to do wrong
in the end you will answer to Him.

Chapter IV

JESUS CHRIST

"No man can follow *Christ* and go astray."

William H. P. Faunce 1859 –1930

A Christmas Present

Matthew 2:1-11

A shining star led wise men
on the road to Bethlehem
Where a baby lay in a manger
all part of God's glorious plan [1]

This baby's name was Jesus
God's gift to you and me [2]
Born to a virgin named Mary
to help us grow spiritually

In time He showed us how to live
to resist society's wrongs
Follow God's Word, do what God says
do this and you will remain strong

Jesus is God's begotten Son [3]
our present, God's glorious gift
We honor by celebrating His birth
on December the 25th

This is our Christian holiday
a love-giving time of the year
Presents appear to be everywhere
and red is the color to wear

People enjoy decorating homes,
we see Christmas trees covered with lights
The Spirit of love enriching the air
as everything seems just right

But when we celebrate we must not forget
the *true meaning* of this Christian day
Always thank God for the gift He gave
to show Him obey Him, and pray.

[1] Luke 2:7-17   [2] Isaiah 9:6   [3] John 3:16

King of Kings

1 Timothy 6:15

As we journey into the Word of God
in time we will certainly find
There was only one who walked on this earth
fully human and fully divine [1]

He entered this world born to a virgin
yes, He was the Chosen One
God made this clear when He spoke these words
"This is my beloved Son" [2]

Jesus performed great miracles
feeding thousands with fish and bread [3]
Water to wine, sight to the blind, [4]
some witnessed Him raise the dead [5]

He warned beware of false teachers
their words they want us to believe
And always watch out for the evil one
with its tricks to keep us deceived

Jesus is also the head of the church
the foundation, the centerpiece
Where believers gather to worship God
and to learn God's Word when preached

He has been called a teacher from God [6]
such wisdom had never been heard
Some religious leaders did not feel the same
they thought of Him more as absurd

He chose twelve men to follow Him [7]
disciples is what they were called
Then taught them about salvation
and to go share this good news with all

He is our Savior and Redeemer
and He showed us how to live good
He paid the debt for all our sins
in a way that no one else could

Jesus knew what no one else knew
from the moment His life begun
His message was clear for all to hear
"I and the Father are one" [8]

No one compares to Jesus Christ
His wisdom should not be ignored
Not only was He called King of kings
but He also was Lord of lords.

[1] John 1:14   [2] Matthew 17:5   [3] Mark 6:38-44
[4] John 2:7-11   [5] John 11:40-44   [6] John 3:2
[7] Matthew 10:2-4   [7] Luke 6:13-16   [7] Mark 3:16-19
[8] John 10:30

He Showed Us How

Luke 9:23-25

This journey called life is no easy task
it is unique and one of a kind
Free will allows us to live as we choose
as thoughts occupy our minds

Thoughts arrive in various forms
the bad ones can lead us astray
God knowing this chose to send His Son
to show us how to live the right way

Jesus told of the Kingdom of God
the place we should to strive to be
But to enter depends on how we live
whom we follow, and with whom we agree

He taught us how to communicate
with God and how we are to pray [1]
Follow God's Word and do what He said
stay humble and always obey

He was our example of how we are to serve
and be willing to serve anytime [2]
He willingly did what the Father said
although He was fully divine

His concern and compassion for everyone
our model of how we are to love
A spiritual lesson for us to learn
from our Heavenly Father above

He chose to forgive those who wronged Him
and did it without a fuss
And reminded us we must do the same
as God keeps forgiving us

He warned us about material things
earthly treasures can lead us to greed
We are to store our treasures in Heaven [3]
if it is God we are longing to please

He didn't have much but the clothes on His back
and no place to rest His head [4]
His teaching and wisdom was all that mattered
to ensure we are spiritually fed

He showed us how He handled temptation
when evil confronted Him [5]
By protecting Himself with the Word of God
our strength to resisting sin

He was very clear we should always thank God
for all in life we have acquired
And keep in mind to whom much is given
much will be required

Yes Jesus told and showed us how
God wants us to live and do right
And for all who choose to live as He did
you will find on the *Path to the Light.*

[1] Matthew 6:9-13   [2] Mark 10:45   [3] Matthew 6:19-21
[4] Luke 9:58   [5] Matthew 4:1

The Last Supper

Matthew 26:14-30
Mark 14:10-26　　　　　　Luke 22:3-23

On the day before Jesus *gave* His life
Judas went to the Chief Priest and said
"What will you give me for Jesus?"
Thirty pieces of sliver he received then fled

Jesus knew what Judas had done
as His disciples all gathered with Him
They ate and drank not knowing His fate
Lord Jesus would soon be condemned

"Truly, one of you shall betray me"
this Jesus said as He spoke out
"Surely you don't mean me, Lord?"
came from each disciple's mouth

"It is he who dips into this dish
and he knows who he has informed
As it is written I have to go
but for him its best he'd not been born"

Judas then looked at Jesus and said
"Master, please tell me, is it I?"
Jesus looked back and said to him
 "Thou hast said," this is all Jesus replied

As Jesus took bread, He gladly gave thanks
then gave each disciple a piece
Saying, *"This is my body I give to you*
do this in remembrance of me"

"Drink from it, all of you" He said
as He gave His cup to them
*"This is my blood the covenant
which is poured out for forgiveness of sins"*

Then off to the Mount of Olives they went
singing hymns along the way
The disciples together with Jesus Christ
on the eve of man's darkest day.

Man's Darkest Day

Mark 15:6-39

Matthew 27:1-54   Luke 23:1-47   John 19:1-36

An innocent man was accused of a crime
but no fault was found in this man
Foolish cries for His demise
align with a sinister plan

They marched Him down a beaten path
stuck a crown of thorns on His head
He struggled to carry the weight of the world
with the foresight to see Himself dead

They nailed Him high up on a cross
then darkness commanded the sky
While paying the price for all our sins
He released His own Spirit, "good-bye"

Some felt sorrow while looking at Him
but before His life was all through
He raised His head to the Father and said,
"Forgive them for they know not what they do"

With His last breath a big earthquake came
and the impact hit all very hard
Then a Roman soldier looked at him and said,
"This truly was the Son of God"

This was our Savior, Jesus Christ
on the day He was crucified
No greater love can one ever show
than for *you* to be willing to die

                              (but …

(The Resurrection)

Mark 16:1-19
Matthew 28:1-20   Luke 24:1-52   John 20:1-29

...darkness can never overcome Light
this is not how this story ends
Jesus *chose* to lay down His life [1]
for the purpose of bearing our sins [2]

Jesus fulfilled the Father's will [3]
as He paid the ultimate price
For us who *believe* to be with Him
in God's everlasting paradise)

Then Jesus was taken down from the cross
to a borrowed tomb Joseph owned
But on the third day when Mary returned
an angel had rolled back the stone

Jesus's body was no longer there
He arose just like He said
Jesus was walking and talking to folks
because Jesus was no longer dead

Jesus appeared before His disciples
and assured them He was no fraud
Then He ascended to Heaven above [4]
and now sits at the right hand of God.

[1] John 10:17-18   [2] 1 Corinthians 15:3-4   [3] Luke 22:42
[4] Acts 1:9

Gave You My All

John 10:14-15

Many have said they know who I AM
but Me you do not recognize [1]
I tried to reveal Myself to you
but you *choose* remain unwise

Some have tried to show you My Words
they put them right in your view
But you made it clear you did not have time
you had something more important to do

At times I would send you messages
I would put them right in your ear
But you would not listen to what I'd say
you pretended like you did not hear

I gave you My all in sacrifice
I underwent so much pain
All this to place you in a position
so you'd be the one who would gain

But your mind is focused on worldly things
blinders are blocking your sight
Temptation keeps drawing you into darkness
and further away from My Light

Time is quickly running out
like others, please come follow Me
I am the way, the truth, and the life [2]
I'm the right path to eternity

Together in Heaven I want us to be
so please come submit to My call
If you disobey and go your own way
I know that I gave you My all.

[1] John 1:10   [2] John 14:6

Chapter V

The (HOLY) SPIRIT

"Life is a journey, and we can't lead ourselves to the destination when we have no idea what or where it is. Let the *Holy Spirit* guide you."

Unknown

The Helper

John 14:16

Life all should know is a gift from God
we experience everyday
Along with this gift we have been warned
temptation is coming our way [1]

Temptation is sly, <u>it</u> creeps in our minds
then strongly suggests what we need
These are the times we truly need help
to make sure <u>it</u> does not succeed

Long ago when folks needed help
they had Jesus, God's begotten Son
Temptation could not bring Him to His knees
because He was the Chosen One

Before Jesus left He told of the Helper
whom the Father was going to send
To equip believers with spiritual strength [2]
and the knowledge of how to defend [3]

The Helper's been called a Comforter,
an Advocate, Counselor, and more
He reminds us we are to live by God's Word
this is how we spiritually mature

This Helper is known as the Holy Spirit
He is one in the Trinity
And when He comes to dwell in us [4]
we will learn to live differently

The Spirit of God comes to live in those
who truly believe and confess
Jesus is Lord, He died, and He rose
the Helper they then will possess

By the Holy Spirit believers are sealed [5]
as God calls each one His own
We are His children who walk in the Light
with God's Spirit we are never alone.

[1] James 1:13-15   [2] Ephesians 3:16   [3] John 16:13-15
[4] John 14:17   [5] Ephesians 1:13-14

Don't Lie to Me

Acts 5:1-11

Why is it some folks would rather lie
than be honest and tell the truth
Here is a warning why lying is wrong
let me give you some Biblical proof

This is a story of husband and wife
the price they both had to pay
As they *willingly* lied to the Holy Spirit
and thought they could get away

Ananias and his wife Sapphira
chose to lie because of their greed
Convincing themselves they deserved more
when God was fulfilling their needs

Peter asked both, "Why do you lie,
did you let Satan fill your heart?"
"Withholding some money for yourselves?"
they had to know this was not smart

Ananias fell down and quickly died
then two men carried him out
Sapphira lied then fell and died too
from the words that came out of her mouth

When we *choose* to lie we do what God hates
for the purpose is just to deceive
The serpent devised this scheme long ago
in the garden when talking to Eve

Always remember lies come with a price
and some at a great expense
So if you decide on purpose to lie
be prepared for the consequence.

Spiritual Fruit

Galatians 5:19-23

Our earthly desires are dangerous
they produce negativity
Envy, hatred, lust, and more
all lead to indecency

But there is a way to avoid all this
in life and it is not hard
Learn to live with the *fruit of the Spirit*
submit and give your life to God

Show others the *love* God has shown you
we are told this again and again
The blessings of *joy* you too will enjoy
as God's Spirit indwelling begins

The calmness of *peace* will come in your life
at times when you feel unsure
Longsuffering teaches you God is at work
be patient, stay strong, and endure

Approach other people with *gentleness*
be *kind* to your fellow man
Goodness is how you imitate God
in your effort to follow His plan

Faith in God is the core belief
let it root deep within your heart
Your strength for maintaining *self-control*
when things in your life fall apart

These are the seeds of spiritual fruit
believers are blessed to receive
Implant them to grow your spiritual life
and convey what you truly believe

Spiritual fruit is good for your soul
this will raise you to a new height
Providing you spiritual nourishment
when you are exposed to the Light

You too can receive this spiritual fruit
and your life can become anew
Will you be deceived by your earthly desires
or enjoy this fruit God has for you?

Spiritually Connected

1 John 4:7-13

Give me your hands
now close your eyes
Let me take you to a place
that will have you mesmerized

Listen closely to my voice
and feel the warmth of my hands
Go deep inside yourself
obey your spiritual demands

We are entering this place
that you have never been
You will learn and be amazed
by your spirit life within

See the fountain of your soul
don't be afraid take a sip
Taste the power of your spirit
this is no ordinary trip

Explore this new world
how God meant for life to be
When two people are in love
and connected spiritually

As our spirits come together
feel true love the way God planned
Not the way love is defined
by the carnal minded man

This is not about sex
this is the bonding of two souls
You cannot put a price on this
and it's worth more than any gold

The best gift two could ever have
and it's given from up above
Is being spiritually connected
and understanding God is love.

Spiritual Warfare

Ephesians 6:10-13

This battle continues every day
and we are all running out of time
Make no mistake how important this is
understand this battle is for our minds

Demonic forces are after us
their tactics are very bold
We possess something they desperately want
they long to imprison our souls

I'm talking about a spiritual war
where demons are fighting for keeps
Please do not think they will ever stop
they are attacking us while we are sleep

They need to see us disobey God
to do what we know is wrong [1]
So we'll be condemned in Hell with them
to a tormented life that's prolonged

It tempted our Lord in the wilderness
to bow down and all would be His [2]
Jesus was pure and much too strong
without Jesus we surely will give

Paul provided some help for us
he explained this battle is hard
The only way to prepare every day
is to put on the whole armor of God

Now you may believe whatever you want
and *think* this is no big deal
You have been warned; prepare yourself
because spiritual warfare is real.

[1] Romans 2:8-9   [2] Matthew 4:1-11

Prepare for Battle

Ephesians 6:14-18

Each day there is an endless battle
for our minds we cannot see
Against wickedness in very high places
this is happening spiritually

The disciple Paul tries to warn us
to be ready so we can stand strong
The example he gives to help us relate
is a Roman soldier's uniform

This is how we prepare ourselves
from the tricks of the devil each day
We must put on *the whole armor of God*
if not we'll end up as its prey

The belt of truth is how we begin
add *the breastplate of righteousness*
Our feet equipped with *the gospel of peace*
this allows us to stand at our best

We hold on tight to *the shield of faith*
from the moment we're ready to start
This is how we defend ourselves
from those fiery wicked darts

We cover our heads at all times
with *the helmet of salvation*
The sword of the spirit, the Word of God
protects us from evil temptations

With this and prayer we ask God for help
we know only He can provide
On all occasions we remember to pray
God's people will all survive

As long as we stay in union with Christ
we can handle what evil brings
Because we have been told we have the strength
and through Christ we can do all things [1]

So now we know what we are to do
especially when things get hard
The only way we can withstand evil
is to put on *the whole armor of God.*

[1] Philippians 4:13

Chapter VI

PRAYER

"*Prayer* requires more of the heart than of the tongue."

Adam Clarke 1760-1832

Heavenly Bound

Ezekiel 3:12

I have just moved up
to a higher level in life
God has shown me how
to handle strife

My friends are all talking
and my relatives too
How I've changed my old ways
and I'm enjoying the new

No longer do I see things
in those negative ways
Since I got on my knees
and began to pray

I prayed and asked God
to please keep me strong
Help me to resist
when I think of doing wrong

God answered my prayers
and many can see
Because now the Holy Spirit
dwells within me

God gave me the strength
and changed my heart
I want to do God's will
and fulfill my part

Far too many times
I have failed in the past
But now God and I
are together at last

See I am a model
of what God's grace can do
When you pray and obey
God will change your life too.

My Secret Place

Matthew 6:6

There is a place I can go
yet to others this place is unknown
No one else can enter this place
but I know here I'm never alone

Whenever I choose to enter this place
no one is able to see
I can relax and be myself
here I know in my heart I am free

Free from all the worldly things
meant to steer my focus away
This is the place I take the time out
seek God and begin to pray

I thank God for all He has done in my life
acknowledging how much I am blessed
His positive shield in this negative world
allows me to stay at my best

Deep in my heart I am true to Him
daily I make sure He knows
When I'm in His presence I bow to Him
great respect for God at His throne

Often I love to give God praise
for in Him I can always confide
Assured and knowing deep in my heart
I always have God on my side.

Special Bread

Luke 11:1-4

Whenever the body hungers for food
it surely will let us know
When it is time for us to eat
food's required to physically grow

Food is the body's nourishment
to live, it's an absolute need
But our spirit thrives on a different supply
and requires a special feed

This type of feeding is known as prayer
our spirit needs it everyday
As the Holy Spirit intercedes for us [1]
to God when He hears us pray

Jesus taught us how to pray
this is how we communicate
And draw ourselves closer to God
whom we love and appreciate

Jesus Christ is the bread of life
through Him we will hunger no more [2]
We need to obey and follow His Word
He's the key to our heavenly door

Our bodies require food every day
to stay healthy and move ahead
The way to grow a well-nourished spirit
is each day with some "Special Bread."

[1] Romans 8:26-27   [2] John 6:35

Prayer Menu

Philippians 4:6

Prayer is how we communicate
with God who created us all
We open to Him, express how we feel
especially at times when we fall

Here is a list of several prayers
which I'd like to share with you
One or more you will have need for
as you look at this prayer menu

The *prayer of petition* is asking God
He said this can be achieved [1]
But we are to pray with a thankful heart
so our request God will receive

Intercessory prayer is unselfishness
we're to pray for others we know
Even for those who have done us wrong
in the Bible it is written so [2]

The *prayer of confession* is telling the truth
admitting to God our sins [3]
Asking God for forgiveness and strength
as we try not to do wrong again

In the *prayer of thanksgiving* we recognize
God again has answered our prayer [4]
He's blessed us once more like He has before
His love shows us how much He cares

Adoration prayer is all about God
who we often praise and adore [5]
To show Him love and worship Him
as His reign lasts forevermore

These prayers have the right ingredients
they are good nourishment for your soul
Each will address a specific need
and fulfills an important role

This menu of prayers will satisfy
your spiritual appetite
These are a few ways to connect with God
as you travel the *Path to the Light*.

[1] 1 John 5:14-15 [2] Matthew 5:44 [3] Psalms 32:5
[4] Colossians 4:2 [5] Psalms 103:1-4

Just Ask

John 15:7

The Bible teaches us many things
like how God wants us to live
If we obey and follow God's Word
we will receive what God's *willing* to give

Jesus said, and all can read
"Ask, and you shall receive" [1]
You do not have because you do not ask [2]
but to ask first you have to believe [3]

For us to believe we must have faith
and trust what God said will come true
There cannot be any doubt in our mind [4]
and our thinking must become anew

We start by thanking God when we pray
for His love, His mercy, His grace
Acknowledging all He has done in our life
as His Word and His will we embrace

God's Word is clear, *"If you abide in Me*
and My Word abides in you
Then you shall ask whatever you wish
and it shall be done for you"

We who read and study God's Word
understand what this asking means
This is not about asking for anything
and we know not to ask as routine

God always knows what is not in our life
we are told He'll supply all our needs ⁵
But *stop* right here, let's be very clear
our *need* does not mean our greed

The most important thing when we ask
please always keep this in mind
If we obey and do what God said
our answer will come in God's time.

¹ Matthew 7:7   ² James 4:2-3   ³ Mark 11:24
⁴ Mark 11:23   ⁵ Philippians 4:19

Answering Prayers

Matthew 21:22

Why hasn't God answered my prayers?
a friend asked me this question one day
In an effort to help him understand
I answered his question this way

God can answer anyone's prayers
yet it is always done in God's time
But do we do what God tells us to?
just a thought we should keep in mind

The Bible tells us to give God the praise,
the honor, and always the glory [1]
The great commission says preach the Gospel [2]
go out and tell all of God's story

Do we study God's Word to show we are approved,
have faith, obey, and believe?
Do we forgive others as God forgives us?
this is hard, but this we must achieve

Are *God's commandments* part of our life [3, 4]
the way God said we are to live?
When others need help and come to us
how much of ourselves do we give? [5]

Have we transformed and renewed our minds [6]
do we humble ourselves before God?
Have we repented and turned from sin
which we know without God is so hard?

God answers prayers however He wants
as He listens to our requests
He may say *yes*, have us *wait* or say *no*
God always knows for us what's best

You are waiting on God to answer your prayers
this we know God surely can do
But have you ever *stopped* for a minute to *think*
maybe God is waiting on you?

[1] Daniel 4:34   [2] Matthew 28:16-20   [3] Exodus 20:1-17
[4] Matthew 22:34-40 [5] Philippians 2:4   [6] Romans 12:2

Chapter VII

CHRISTIAN FAITH

"To one who has *faith*, no explanation is necessary
To one without *faith*, no explanation is possible."

Thomas Aquinas, 1225-1274

Faith Believers

Hebrews 11:1-39

Without faith we cannot please God
now let me explain what faith means
Faith is the substance of things we hope for
and the evidence of things not seen

The Bible tells us of several people
whom God took a liking to
In Hebrews 11 this is recorded
their accounts I now share with you

Abel offered his best to God [1]
Enoch, God took him away [2]
Noah heard God and built the Ark [3]
Abraham left home and obeyed [4]

Sarah, though old, finally conceived [5]
Isaac blessed both of his sons [6]
Jacob blessed Joseph's sons the same way [7]
with Joseph's bones the journey begun [8]

Moses' parents hid him from Pharaoh [9]
God's promise to Moses was real [10]
Rahab hid Israelite spies at her home [11]
and there is more the Bible reveals

Each was moved by the Spirit of God
and their faith led them to succeed
They trusted God, they did what He said
this showed how in God they believed

These are a few I have written about
and there are others who obeyed the same
They all have a special place in Heaven
some refer to as God's Faith Hall of Fame.

[1] Genesis 4:4   [2] Genesis 5:24   [3] Genesis 6:14
[4] Genesis 12:1   [5] Genesis 18:9-15   [6] Genesis 27:27-40
[7] Genesis 48:14-20   [8] Genesis 50:25   [9] Exodus 2:1-3
[10] Exodus 3:16-17   [11] Joshua 2:3-4

Christian Doctrine

1 Timothy 4:6

Religion is based on what one believes
the faith one has in their heart
With all the religions in the world
one's belief is what sets us apart

Christians have faith and truly believe
the Words of the Bible are true
The Scriptures are God's infallible Words
they tell us what we are to do

Christians believe in the Trinity
the three roles of how our God exists
The Father, The Son, The Holy Spirit
true Christians believe in this

God, the Father, created all
He rules over everything
Humans, animals, plants, the earth,
and the supernatural unseen

We are created in the image of God [1]
we are physical and spiritual beings
And when we *choose* to disobey God
we experience all kinds of bad things

Jesus, God's Son, was born of a virgin
He died for all of our sins
Then after three days He rose from the grave
to walk on this earth again

Jesus is also the head of our church [2]
where we go to worship and pray
And sharpen each other in fellowship [3]
see, we spiritually grow this way

The Holy Spirit is God's gift
to all who confess and believe
He reminds us how we are to live
and can stay with us permanently

Other religions have their own beliefs
each practice their own creed
But this is the doctrine we hold in our hearts
this is what true Christians believe.

[1] Genesis 1:27   [2] Colossians 1:18   [3] Proverbs 27:17

Christian Walk

2 Corinthians 5:7

Christians have faith in the Bible
God's Word we believe this to be
We walk by faith and not by sight
to grow righteous and spiritually

We trust in God with all our hearts
lean not on what we understand [1]
God will direct our path through life
when we choose to live by His plan

We have been told to study God's Word
to show ourselves approved
Transform our minds from sinful thoughts
so our old self can then be removed

Humble ourselves to help one another
this is how God wants us to live
Share the good news of Jesus Christ
and the love He told us to give

We give our all to Jesus Christ
confess with our mouths and believe [2]
And as we yield to the Holy Spirit
there is much in life we will achieve

We have been warned of the devil's attacks
his temptation can make our life hard
But God provides protection for us
when we put on the whole armor of God

This Christian walk is no easy walk
our faith will be put to the test
Problems are coming into our lives
we are going to have to address

As we remain connected to God
we will spiritually comprehend
The importance of being in tune with God
to receive the signals He sends

We are warned of those who preach
of material prosperity
How they purposely avoid scripture context
with their unbiblical reality

Many will have you *think* they are Christians
based on their Christian-like talk [3]
But only a few God will consent
come in line with a true Christian walk.

[1] Proverbs 3:5-6   [2] Romans 10:9-10   [3] 1 John 4:1

The Struggle

Galatians 5:16-26

These two are at it once again
in their ongoing tug-of-war
All are concerned who will win
because the outcome's forevermore

The stakes in this war are very high
these opponents have powerful roles
The Flesh and the Spirit remain at odds
for the winner will gain full control [1]

The Flesh is our body given to us
humans are each given one
We are born into this sinful world [2]
and enjoy what we *think* is fun

But the Spirit cannot live this way
being part of the Trinity
When the Spirit comes to dwell in you
you will learn how to live more Godly

This is the life Christians must live
we experience this everyday
The Spirit reveals how we are to live
but the Flesh still prefers the old way [3]

Non-believers look at some Christians and say,
"See, I told you they're hypocrites"
Based on what they see us do
but there is something they just do not get

They do not understand our struggle inside
and change, we all know, is hard
But we know this pain is worth the gain
as we are moving closer to God

This struggle I tell you will never end
this is deeper than many can see
For the winner determines where we will spend
our spiritual eternity.

[1] Romans 8:5-6   [2] Galatians 3:22   [3] Matthew 26:41

When God Calls You

Jonah 1:1-17

There will come a time in your life
that you may not quite understand
This difficult time you must undergo
will be God and Him working His plan

This is when God is calling you
and for many this time will be hard
There is no way to get around this
when you are one on one with God

God is trying to help you become
the person He wants you to be
So you may learn your purpose in life
and move on to your true destiny

God knows it is not easy for you
to move from your comfort zone
Just trust in God to show you the way
He said He wouldn't leave you alone [1]

This encounter you will never win
from the day God starts calling on you
Jonah thought he could run from God
remember all that he went through

When you submit you will see God work
your life will undergo change
The more you choose to follow God's will
others may view you as strange

When God calls you this is a good thing
there is something God has planned for you
He will provide you with what you need
and His Word verifies this is true

Now you may ask, why I believe,
and others with you may agree
God gave me the wisdom to write this book
see, I listened when God called me.

[1] Deuteronomy 31:6

More Than a Sermon

Matthew 5:1-2

We go to church to hear God's Word
to learn what God has to say
The Preacher interprets the Bible for us [1]
and explains why we need to obey

God's Word gives us strength so we may cope
with the trials of life we go through [2]
We learn about faith, peace, love, and joy
the importance of being renewed

But there is more to learning God's Word
than the sermons we go and attend
Like Sunday school and Bible study
they help nurture our spirit within

These classes are held and teachers explain
God's Word in further detail
Questions are asked, comments are made
interaction helps all to prevail

In Sunday school, we learn about life
the values we all should uphold
Why not to do wrong, what's morally right,
submit and let God take control

Bible study is always a plus
here we learn of historical facts
People, traditions, cultures, timelines
and explore Biblical maps

As our knowledge of God continues to grow
from the lessons in class we receive
God's wisdom teaches us to understand [3]
what to others we say we believe

God's Word is clear how we are to live
there is no need to second guess
Why it is important to focus on God
so we'll be right when it's time to confess

These classes are held to empower us
in ways like nothing else can
Sermons are good but no questions are asked
and I've never seen one raise their hand

If deep in your heart you want to learn more
you're sincere and very determined
Go in and attend a Bible class
because there is more to God's Word than a sermon.

[1] 1 Peter 4:11   [2] James 1:2-5   [3] Acts 8:30-31

Chapter VIII

ANGELS & DEMONS

"It was pride that changed *angels* into *demons*."

Saint Augustine 354-430

Spiritual Messengers

Revelation 12:7-8

God chose to place humans here on earth
in a world where much can be seen
He intended for us to enjoy life
as physical and spiritual beings [1]

Our spiritual side cannot be seen
this everyone should know is true
This is where we connect with God
Holy angels are there with God too

Angels like man were created by God
yet God made them higher than man
They possess superior intelligence
they are immortal and have no life span [2]

Only God knows how many He has
they are numbered like the stars in the sky [3]
They praise and follow God's every command
God's Word they obey and comply

These angels are spiritual messengers [4]
God sends them to minister to us
They love to rejoice when we become saved
and repent from the sins of our lust

They are invisible to the human eye
yet at times, God's had some appear [5]
The Bible tells they resemble man
but God they prefer to be near

They are also known as heavenly hosts
God created them differently
Each has a divine position
in God's celestial hierarchy

But not all the angels chose to serve God
this is an important fact
Heavenly angels do what God says
fallen angels *choose* us to attack

They lost their holiness long ago
when God they chose to defy [6]
They willingly followed Satan instead
so like him they fell from the sky [7]

Now they are known as Satan's demons
they do not want to see us do well
They are out to deceive and destroy our lives
so we will end up tormented in Hell

Angels are spiritual messengers
forever they will be around
Take notice when things happen in your life
their messages are very profound.

[1] John 3:6   [2] Luke 20:36   [3] Revelation 5:11
[4] Hebrews 1:14   [5] Judges 6:11-12 [6] 2 Peter 2:4
[7] Luke 10:18

Angel Talk

Luke 1:19

I talked to an angel many years ago
though unaware at the time
He spoke two words of wisdom to me
that forever have stayed in my mind

The way he came and conversed with me
at that time seemed somewhat odd
But what I did not know back then
is he came with a message from God

He said we need to understand
this world in which we live
To help me with my journey through life
these two words to me he did give

First is the word *interpretation*
"How does one interpret things?"
If what we conceive is not based in truth
what result do you think it will bring?

We all can agree the glass is half
but dispute whether empty or full
The things we experience in our lives
will have some directional pull

Next he spoke of our *purpose*
he asked, "Do you know why you're here?"
In the book of Ecclesiastes
King Solomon makes this quite clear

"Fear God, and keep His commandments
for this is the whole duty of man" [1]
King Solomon ends his book this way
providing his wisdom firsthand

The angel shared this message with me
then departed and went on his way
This knowledge is too important to keep
so I share this with all today.

[1] Ecclesiastes 12:13

In the Den

1 John 5:19

This is the place that welcomes you
where you *think* you are at your best
Here you can do whatever you choose
as you journey through your life's quest

The voice you hear encouraging you
mistakenly sounds like a friend
You need be aware of where you are
you are now in the devil's den

This is the place you do not want to be
at first all seems to be good
Enjoying life the way you want
but there is something you misunderstood

There is an evil spirit influencing you
that you are unable to see [1]
Suggesting to you to do what you want
with its deceitful strategy

There are consequences ahead of you
with a price you will have to pay
For doing the things you *know* are wrong
and determining to have things your way

Now you may believe you are in control
but you truly have been deceived
The devil has placed you where he wants
sin now is all you *will* receive

So if you decide to stay in the den
and continue the things you do
Be assured your father gladly waits
and to Hell he will welcome you.

[1] 2 Corinthians 4:4

Beware of Evil
1 Peter 5:8

<u>It</u> is like a disease that will not leave
its purpose it loves and enjoys
<u>It</u> is out to wreak havoc on everyone's life
and won't stop until all are destroyed [1]

I'm talking about the evil spirit
which is known by many names
Lucifer, Satan, devil, serpent
stay alert, they're all one and the same [2]

We need to go back to where <u>it</u> began
this was long before Adam and Eve
<u>It</u> first appeared in Heaven near God
in an angel who focused on greed

Lucifer was once a Cherubim angel
who had access to God at His throne
His beauty, wisdom, and awesome power
other angels would love to have owned

But Lucifer became obsessed with God
God's power he wanted to feel
So Lucifer's pride made <u>it</u> come alive
<u>it is evil</u>, <u>it</u> lives, and <u>it</u>'s real

"I will" he professed several times
evil had him believe he could win [3]
So Lucifer rebelled and disobeyed God
but to disobey God is a sin

He swayed many angels to follow him
they rejected what God had to say
They chose to follow evil instead
so like evil God cast them away [4]

As fallen angels their roles have changed
and so has the place where they dwell
Now they are known as Satan's demons
their new mission is to drag us to Hell

Satan's extremely powerful
he knows how to charm with delight
Satan has even transformed himself
to look like an *angel of light* [5]

Evil is not a person or thing
it's a spirit that seeks to control
Evil we must know has nothing to lose
this is why evil will always be bold

Evil is cunning and very bright
it knows how to make us comply
By telling us just what we want to hear
because evil's the father of lies [6]

Evil can get into anyone's head
our families, our lovers, and friends
By jealousy, doubt, disbelief, lies,
then deceit and destruction move in

Evil enjoys confusing us
this warning please never forget
It needs to see us disobey God
and do it without any regret

Evil may leave for a little while
but if it can't find a new place to rest
It will return with seven worse friends [7]
to make sure our lives are a mess

Evil loves to manipulate us
by the ways it strongly suggests
But evil *can't make* us do anything
because evil's humanly powerless

At no time will evil fear us
but it fears our ability
The power we have with the Word of God
resist evil; you will see it flee. [8]

[1] John 10:10 [2] Revelation 12:9 [3] Isaiah 14:13-14
[4] Matthew 25:41 [5] 2 Corinthians 11:14 [6] John 8:44
[7] Luke 11:24-26 [8] James 4:7

The Final Judgment

Revelation 20:11-15

When all is done and our life on earth
has finally come to an end
There will be a trial that will take place
to judge secrets, good deeds, and sins [1]

This will be known as Judgment Day
those who do not believe will be there
To stand in front of the *great white throne*
for the verdict you do not want to hear

Books will be opened on this day
your life will be read to you
Records of your entire life
all your rights and all your wrongs too

Last will be read the *book of life*
now pray that you hear your name
Not all who say they believe in God [2]
will encounter a heavenly gain

For all the names that are not called
there is a second death waiting for them
They'll be cast into the *lake of fire*
where their torment will never end

This poem should always remind us
to live life in a Godly way
Since every knee shall bow and tongue confess [3]
before Him on Judgment Day.

[1] Ecclesiastes 12:14   [2] Matthew 7:21   [3] Romans 14:11

Chapter IX

WISDOM

"True *wisdom* comes to each of us when we realize how little we understand about life, ourselves, and the world around us."

Socrates 469 BC – 399 BC

Our Greatest Fear

Matthew 7:23

Feelings control our emotional state
they have an enormous impact
Governed by what we see and hear
this determines how we will react

Some are good and some are bad
it is all in the way they appear
The feeling I choose to talk about
is a dominant one we call fear

Fear will alter the way we think
it can scare us right away
As it takes control of us mentally
and uses our mind as its prey

Everyone has experienced fear
it appears in various forms
Sometimes we bring fear on ourselves
then it takes us right out of our norm

Fear makes us feel something's not right
but we don't know to what degree
Our spirit warns us be vigilant
as we are altered emotionally

But the greatest fear we could ever have
this no one should want to go through
Is on Judgment Day to hear God say,
"Depart from me, I never knew you."

Our Life, God's Plan

Jeremiah 29:11

Our life is a precious gift from God
the journey is one of a kind
The day we begin to follow God's plan
the truth about life we will find

Then we will see like never before
how we have been living a lie
Deceiving orders were given to us
lack of knowledge caused us to comply

An unfriendly spirit leads us to do wrong
tricking us not to do what is right
Misguiding us from the Giver of life
into darkness away from the Light

We *choose* the immoral life to live [1]
feeling others we have to impress
Bonding with those who don't care about us
then complain how our lives are a mess

Finding ourselves quick to complain
how in life we have it so hard
As we listen to others and do what they want
disobeying the Word of God

God gives us power to live how we please
by the choices we make everyday
He gave us free will and His Word
then waits to see who will obey

When we focus our lives on God's plan
a new way of life we will see
Then we will move in the right direction
onward to our true destiny

Yes, God has a plan waiting for us
outside of the realm of sin
In relationship with Jesus Christ [2]
where His Spirit indwelling begins

A peaceful world created by God
here we no longer want to complain
God's Word lets us know: He is in control
and His love keeps us safe as He reigns

We are living our lives the way we want
but we clearly do not understand
This journey called life is not about us
it's about God; learn to live as He planned.

[1] 1 John 2:15-16   [2] 1 John 3:23-24

Listen to the Lord

Proverbs 22:17-19

If we listen to the Lord
and hear what He has to say
We will come to realize
there is a much better way

This is really very simple
and I'll tell you how to start
All you do is take His Word
and plant within your heart

The Lord is always talking
and He tells us what to do
Yet we think we know what's better
later finding that's not true

We choose to follow others
those who spirits are not right
They don't listen to the Lord
and with God, they won't unite

God knows we are not perfect
and He knows we'll make mistakes
This is part of being human
so His mercy gives us breaks

God warns us of temptation
and <u>it</u> wants to pull us in
We should listen to His Word
so we do not fall to prey to sin

God's Word is here to help us
and to keep us on His course
When we listen to His Spirit
we recognize the evil force

We must listen to the Lord
there is much we need to know
Because His Word clearly warns us
we will reap what we sow. [1]

[1] Galatians 6:7

Free Will

Joshua 24:14-15

Imagine a child in a position
where they are totally in control
The power of choice to do right or wrong
and truly enjoying this role

In a short time they start to believe
they have no one to answer to
To make matters worse, search deep in your heart
because this child I write of is *you*

The power of choice is a God-given gift
Christians know this as free will
When you realize what this truly means
this may start to give you some chills

Almighty God is so powerful
He has given this power to you
Now you can live however you want
but remember God knows all you do [1]

If you *choose* to abuse this power God gives
and decide to go and do wrong
Your outcome will not be favorable
and the penalty will be strong

In other words I will try to explain
let me say this another way
If you misuse this gift from God
there's a price you will have to pay

But God foresaw you would need help
His wisdom knew just what this took
So He gave you His Word, the Holy Bible
His do-right instructional book

Now that you know what free will is
and you freely have been advised
I hope when you choose to do what you want
your choice is to do what is wise.

[1] John 3:19-21

True Peace

Philippians 4:7-9

If peace is what you are looking for
you are undoubtedly at the right place
Just follow this path that leads to the Light
God is waiting for you to embrace [1]

To show you how to live in peace
regardless of what you have heard
From those who have never experienced peace
they know nothing about God's Word

The journey to peace can only begin
when you submit to God's control
Confess Jesus is your Lord and Savior
then live by His Word as you're told

Peace surpasses all understanding
peace will guard your heart and mind
But if you prefer a sinful life
true peace you never will find

The only way peace is obtained
this is absolutely free
The Spirit of God must dwell in you
He's your seal and your guarantee

Peace is a priceless gift from God
you will never be able to buy [2]
Nor can you ever duplicate this
no matter how hard you may try

Peace generates change in your life
and opens your eyes to much more
You'll begin to see the world differently
with calmness like never before

You will learn to appreciate little things
realign your priorities
And realize what is important in life,
God, faith, love, and humanity

Peace will always keep you assured
no matter what you may go through
True peace lets you know you have been blessed
remember who you belong to

Things that used to trouble you
will no longer get you upset
Peace will show you how to stay strong
and not do things you later regret [3]

Many pretend they have true peace
but the truth is there's only a few [4]
Examine their actions when they get upset
their behavior will tell if they're true

If you desire God's gift of peace
let me give you some friendly advice
Take time to learn the Word of God
and live life in union with Christ. [5]

[1] Psalms 18:28-32   [2] Acts 8:18-20   [3] John 14:27
[4] Romans 3:17   [5] 2 Thessalonians 3:16

A Great Secret

Psalms 37:7

There is a great secret given to man
but man has not learned this yet
With all the advancements man has made
this secret, man still does not get

The first thing man must understand
is the word "secret" and just what this means
Keep away from knowledge or views
as in hidden, or let's say unseen

Secrets are in our everyday life
technology makes us comply
Coded passwords, user IDs
without them access is denied

Our way of life has greatly improved
this new world puts us in a race
Our world today moves very fast
and most are enjoying this pace

But is this helping or causing a problem
with our lives spiritually?
Patience many no longer possess
with this get-now mentality

Society says we have to move fast
but that's not what God has to say
Patience is what God requires of us
we must listen to God and obey

No, we should never move before God
just be patient and wait on Him
Because those who get impatient and move
may later find they're indulging in sin

There is a good reason God wants us to wait
and not move ahead and proceed
God may be putting things in place
to ensure we do succeed

The secret man still does not get
I'll tell you and it is not hard
We must be patient, have faith, believe
and learn not to move before God.

Spiritual Delight

Colossians 2:6-7

I heard someone speaking the Word of God
unaware they were planting a seed
Slowly God's Word took root in my mind
curiosity led me to read

I was eager to learn more of God's Word
and what God had to say
So I journeyed into the Holy Bible
I watched as God showed me the way

God's Word conveyed thoughts to my mind
forming questions I began to search
I was told the clergy can answer them
seeking knowledge, I went to the church

As I entered I felt a warm welcoming
from the smile on the greeter's face
When I felt the preacher was talking to me
I knew then I was in the right place

Next I attended Bible class
I realized this was truly a must
As the lessons revealed important facts
of the Scriptures we learned and discussed

I learned how one's disobedience
can turn one from God straight to sin
And the only way to get back to God
is to repent and become born again

In time I began to understand
what the duty of man is about
Fear God and keep His commandments
believe in Him without any doubt

This knowledge has helped me understand
now my wisdom and faith all can see
Whenever I speak on the Word of God
all can tell I've grown spiritually

Spiritual delight is available
for all who want to live right
Now continue your journey into the Bible
after reading *Path to the Light*.

Conclusion

The question confronting us all is not whether we believe, but what, and in whom do we believe?

We all believe in something. Generally speaking, how we live and the things we do are outward expressions of our inner feelings and beliefs. There are, however, some exceptions. People who say or pretend that they are genuine may actually lead us away from their beliefs. In moments of desperation, their true feelings are often revealed.

Now, I ask you the questions: What do you believe? In whom do you believe? Who is guiding your path through life? Where are you going? These are crucial questions that need to be answered. The direction of our life's journey is dependent on these responses.

We sometimes make unwise and risky choices to satisfy our curiosities. With no guidance, direction, or knowledge of where we are going, uncertain outcome or failure ultimately occurs.

Our chances for enjoying a meaningful journey improve when we choose to travel with a guide. The Bible is the map to guide us as we travel through the pages of this book. Its words of inspiration and discovery provide understanding, awareness, and recovery from some of the dangerous paths we choose to travel. The maps in the Bible cover all of the ground on which we walk and will continue to walk in this lifetime. When we have the instructional roadmap for life, we do not have to guess or wonder whether we are proceeding in the right direction. The Bible is filled with vital information to assist us in making wise choices. The Bible also tells us what happened to those who chose destructive paths for their own journeys.

After years of *not* upholding or appreciating the significance of our morals, values, principles, and human compassion, we continually find ourselves confronted with the challenges of a rapidly deteriorating society. We have allowed the fabric of our society to continue to decay and have done nothing to prevent it, while others have been methodically moving forward in darkness with their deceitful agendas. The creation of our new fabric began long ago. It has been interwoven with threads of dishonesty, greed, hatred, selfishness, etc. These threads of deceit have displaced us. So now we find ourselves trapped in a negative spiral that is leading us down various self-destructive paths. These negative paths are moving us further and further away from the Bible, but closer toward experiences with unfavorable results. Have we become so bewildered that we no longer know how to react or approach people when we know something is wrong? Or do we lack any concern at all? We continue to see and hear of horrible crimes, negative attitudes, and careless mentalities, accompanied by selfish and sinful excuses with no fear of repercussions. When will this all end?

The offerings in these pages were intended to give you a sense of calm, reassurance, encouragement, awareness, and hope. I have gone a step further by presenting what is right: the truth, God's Word, and the Bible. This approach will help to better apply these inspirational poems and readings as you journey through life.

It is my hope and prayer that you have *enjoyed* and *learned* from these pages. I also hope that this experience has you feeling more confident and comfortable as you continue your quest through life and engage in your personal study of the Bible. I want you to know that you are not alone in the disappointments and heartaches of life. Others, like myself, have learned from our study of the Bible that God is always with us on every path; *we are not alone.* His Word is a guide and explanation for how we are to proceed along the way. I have shared a process of understanding and enlightenment to the Bible that I hope you will continue practicing in your daily life. May you always remember to take out your map before you take a step down a path: the journey will be sweeter if you *choose* the narrow gate.

The Narrow and Wide Gates

[13] Enter through the narrow gate. For wide is the gate and broad is the road that leads to destruction, and many enter through it.

[14] But small is the gate and narrow the road that leads to life, and only a few find it. (NIV)

Matthew 7:13-14

Glossary

Abide	= to remain in place; to dwell or reside
Angel	= a immortal celestial being; a messenger from God
Bible	= the collection of sacred writings of the Christian religion, comprising the Old and New Testaments
Blessed	= divinely or supremely favored
Christian	= follower of Jesus Christ and His teachings
Church	= a building were Christians worship
Confess	= to admit or make known one's sin to God
Crucified	= to put one to death by nailing or binding the hands and feet to a cross
Deceive	= to mislead by a false appearance or statement
Demon	= an evil supernatural being; an evil spirit
Devil	= the supreme spirit of evil; ruler of Hell; foe to God; Satan
Disciple	= one of the original followers of Jesus
Disobey	= to refuse or fail to follow an order or a rule
Doctrine	= a body of principles presented for a belief, as by a religious group
Dwell	= to live or stay as a permanent resident; reside
Eternity	= time without beginning or end; infinite time
Evil	= morally bad or wrong; wicked
Faith	= belief in God or in the doctrines or teachings of religion:

Glory	= adoration, praise, and thanksgiving offered in worship
God	= the one Supreme Being, the Creator and ruler of the universe
Gospel	= the teachings of Jesus and the apostles; good news
Grace	= a favor rendered by one who need not do so: indulgence
Greed	= an excessive desire to acquire or possess more than what one needs
Heaven	= the abode of God, the angels, and the souls of those who are granted salvation
Hell	= the abode of evil and condemned souls. The place of eternal punishment for the wicked after death
Indwell	= to exist as an animating divine inner spirit, force or principle
Interprets	= to give or provide the meaning of; explain
Jesus	= the beloved Son of God
Lord	= God; Jesus
Mercy	= compassionate treatment, especially of those under one's power; something for which to be thankful
Obey	= to carry out or follow a command, order, or instruction
Praise	= to express a feeling of gratitude to God; worship or glorify
Prayer	= a devout petition to God; a spiritual communion with God
Repent	= to feel such regret for past behavior one changes their life for the better
Righteousness	= morally upright; without guilt or sin
Salvation	= deliverance from the power and penalty of sin; redemption

Satan	= a powerful spiritual being; the chief evil spirit; the great adversary of God and humanity; the devil
Scriptures	= the sacred writings of the Old and/or New Testaments
Sin	= deliberate disobedience to the known will of God
Spiritual	= of, pertaining to, or consisting of spirit.
Temptation	= the act of tempting or the condition of being tempted
Translation	= to change for one language to another language
Trinity	= the union of three divine persons (Father, Son, and Holy Spirit) in one Godhead,
Wisdom	= the ability to discern or judge what is true, right or lasting: insight
Worship	= ceremonies, prayers, or other religious forms by which this love is expressed

Index

CHAPTER I - ABOUT THE BIBLE

Path to the Light   Page...2

    John 1:1-5
    [1] Psalms 16:11
    [2] John 8:12
    [3] Proverbs 4:19
    [4] Ephesians 5:8-11

The Divine Library   Page...4

    Mark 13:31
    [1] Romans 15:4
    [2] 1 John 5:10-12

Bible Translations   Page...6

    2 Peter 1:20-21
    [1] Revelation 22:18-19

Why the Bible   Page...8

    2 Timothy 3:16
    [1] Proverbs 1:7
    [2] Philippians 2:14-15
    [3] James 1:19
    [4] Proverbs 27:20
    [5] Google this

Missing the Word   Page...11

    Luke 6:46
    [1] 1 John 1:7
    [2] Luke 11:28

In Context   **Page…12**

    2 Timothy 3:15
    [1] 2 Timothy 2:15

CHAPTER II - LESSONS FORM THE SCRIPTURES

Noah's Ark   **Page… 17**

    Genesis 6:8-22, 7, 8, 9:1-16

Heavenly Rewards   **Page…18**

    Proverbs 11:18
    [1] 1 Corinthians 9:25
    [2] 1 Thessalonians 2:19
    [3] 2 Timothy 4:8
    [4] James 1:12
    [5] 1 Peter 5:4

Save Me   **Page…20**

    Acts 16:30-31
    [1] Genesis 3:1-5
    [2] Ephesians 5:6
    [3] John 10:9
    [4] 1 John 4:9
    [5] 1 Thessalonians 5:9
    [6] Ephesians 2:8-9
    [7] Acts 3:19

Let It Go   **Page…22**

    Mark 11:25-26
    [1] Romans 12:19
    [2] Romans 3:23
    [3] Matthew 18:21-22
    [4] Colossians 3:13
    [5] Isaiah 30:20

False Teachers   Page...24

    2 Peter 2:1-3
    [1] Mark 13:22-23
    [2] 2 Corinthians 11:13
    [3] Matthew 7:15
    [4] Colossians 2:8
    [5] Romans 16:17-18
    [6] 2 Timothy 4:3-4

CHAPTER III - ALMIGHTY GOD

Our Invisible God   Page...28

    Romans 1:20
    [1] 1 Timothy 1:17
    [2] Psalms 14:1
    [3] 2 Corinthians 4:18

Essence of Life   Page...30

    Matthew 3:16-17
    [1] Isaiah 55:8-9
    [2] Genesis 1, 2
    [3] Philippians 2:8
    [4] John 14:26
    [5] Exodus 3:14

In God's Time   Page...32

    1 Peter 5:6
    [1] Deuteronomy 7:9

God's Oldest Twins   Page...34

    Hebrews 4:16
    [1] Ecclesiastes 7:20
    [2] Titus 3:4-5
    [3] John 1:16

What God Hates   Page...36

    Proverbs 6:16-19

CHAPTER IV - JESUS CHRIST

Christmas Present   Page...40

    Matthew 2:1-11
    [1] Luke 2:7-17
    [2] Isaiah 9:6
    [3] John 3:16

King of Kings   Page...42

    1 Timothy 6:15
    [1] John 1:14
    [2] Matthew 17:5
    [3] Mark 6:38-44
    [4] John 2:7-11
    [5] John 11:40-44
    [6] John 3:2
    [7] Matthew 10:2-4
    [7] Luke 6:13-16
    [7] Mark 3:16-19
    [8] John 10:30

He Showed Us How   Page...44

    Luke 9:23-25
    [1] Matthew 6:9-13
    [2] Mark 10:45
    [3] Matthew 6:19-21
    [4] Luke 9:58
    [5] Matthew 4:1

The Last Supper   Page...46

    Matthew 26:14-30
    Mark 14:10-26
    Luke 22:3-23

Man's Darkest Day   Page...48

    Mark 15:6-39
    Matthew 27:1-54
    Luke 23:1-47
    John 19:1-36

(The Resurrection)   Page...49

    Mark 16:1-19
    Matthew 28:1-20
    Luke 24:1-52
    John 20:1-29
    [1] John 10:17-18
    [2] 1 Corinthians 15:3-4
    [3] Luke 22:42
    [4] Acts 1:9

Gave You My All   Page...50

    John 10:14-15
    [1] John 1:10
    [2] John 14:6

CHAPTER V - THE HOLY SPIRIT

The Helper   Page...54

    John 14:16
    [1] James 1:13-15
    [2] Ephesians 3:16
    [3] John 16:13-15
    [4] John 14:17
    [5] Ephesians 1:13-14

Don't Lie to Me   Page...56

    Acts 5:1-11

Spiritual Fruit   Page...58

    Galatians 5:19-23

Spiritually Connected   Page...60

    1 John 4:7-13

Spiritual Warfare   Page...62

    Ephesians 6:10-13
    [1] Romans 2:8-9
    [2] Matthew 4:1-11

Prepare for Battle   Page...64

    Ephesians 6:14-18
    [1] Philippians 4:13

CHAPTER VI - PRAYER

Heavenly Bound   Page...68

    Ezekiel 3:12

My Secret Place   Page...70

    Matthew 6:6

Special Bread   Page...71

    Luke 11:1-4
    [1] Romans 8:26-27
    [2] John 6:35

Prayer Menu   Page...72

    Philippians 4:6
    [1] 1 John 5:14-15
    [2] Matthew 5:44
    [3] Psalms 32:5
    [4] Colossians 4:2
    [5] Psalms 103:1-4

Just Ask   Page...74

    John 15:7
    [1] Matthew 7:7
    [2] James 4:2-3
    [3] Mark 11:24
    [4] Mark 11:23
    [5] Philippians 4:19

Answering Prayers   Page...76

    Matthew 21:22
    [1] Daniel 4:34
    [2] Matthew 28:16-20
    [3] Exodus 20:1-17
    [4] Matthew 22:34-40

[5] Philippians 2:4
[6] Romans 12:2

CHAPTER VII - CHRISTIAN FAITH

Faith Believers   Page...80

    Hebrews 11:1-39
    [1] Genesis 4:4
    [2] Genesis 5:24
    [3] Genesis 6:14
    [4] Genesis 12:1
    [5] Genesis 18:9-15
    [6] Genesis 27:27-40
    [7] Genesis 48:14-20
    [8] Genesis 50:25
    [9] Exodus 2:1-3
    [10] Exodus 3:16-17
    [11] Joshua 2:3-4

Christian Doctrine   Page...82

    1 Timothy 4:6
    [1] Genesis 1:27
    [2] Colossians 1:18
    [3] Proverbs 27:17

Christian Walk   Page...84

    2 Corinthians 5:7
    [1] Proverbs 3:5-6
    [2] Romans 10:9-10
    [3] 1 John 4:1

The Struggle   Page...86

    Galatians 5:16-26
    [1] Romans 8:5-6
    [2] Galatians 3:22
    [3] Matthew 26:41

When God Calls You   Page...88

    Jonah 1:1-17
    [1] Deuteronomy 31:6

More Than a Sermon   **Page…90**
    Matthew 5:1-2
    [1] 1 Peter 4:11
    [2] James 1:2-5
    [3] Acts 8:30-31

CHAPTER VIII - ANGELS & DEMONS

Spiritual Messengers   Page…94
    Revelation 12:7-8
    [1] John 3:6
    [2] Luke 20:36
    [3] Revelation 5:11
    [4] Hebrews 1:14
    [5] Judges 6:11-12
    [6] 2 Peter 2:4
    [7] Luke 10:18

Angel Talk   Page…96
    Luke 1:19
    [1] Ecclesiastes 12:13

In the Den   Page…98
    1 John 5:19
    [1] 2 Corinthians 4:4

Beware of Evil   Page…100
    1 Peter 5:8
    [1] John 10:10
    [2] Revelation 12:9
    [3] Isaiah 14:13-14
    [4] Matthew 25:41
    [5] 2 Corinthians 11:14
    [6] John 8:44
    [7] Luke 11:24-26
    [8] James 4:7

The Final Judgment   Page...103
    Revelation 20:11-15
    [1] Ecclesiastes 12:14
    [2] Matthew 7:21
    [3] Romans 14:11

CHAPTER IX - WISDOM

Our Greatest Fear   Page...107
    Matthew 7:23

Our Life, God's Plan   Page...108
    Jeremiah 29:11
    [1] 1 John 2:15-16
    [2] 1 John 3:23-24

Listen to the Lord   Page...110
    Proverbs 22:17-19
    [1] Galatians 6:7

Free Will   Page...112
    Joshua 24:14-15
    [1] John 3:19-21

True Peace   Page...114
    Philippians 4:7-9
    [1] Psalms 18:28-32
    [2] Acts 8:18-20
    [3] John 14:27
    [4] Romans 3:17
    [5] 2 Thessalonians 3:16

A Great Secret   Page...116
    Psalms 37:7

Spiritual Delight   Page...118
    Colossians 2:6-7

Appendix A

THE 66 BOOKS OF THE BIBLE

39 OLD TESTAMENT

The Law
Genesis
Exodus
Leviticus
Number
Deuteronomy

History
Joshua
Judges
Ruth
1 Samuel
2 Samuel
1 Kings
2 Kings
1 Chronicles
2 Chronicles
Ezra
Nehemiah
Esther

Poetry
Job
Psalms
Proverbs
Ecclesiastes
Song of Solomon

Major Prophets
Isaiah
Jeremiah
Lamentations
Ezekiel
Daniel

Minor Prophets
Hosea
Joel
Amos
Obadiah
Jonah
Micah
Nahum
Habakkuk
Zephaniah
Haggai
Zechariah
Malachi

27 NEW TESTAMENT

The Gospels
Matthew
Mark
Luke
John

History of the Church
Acts

Paul's Epistles
Romans
1 Corinthians
2 Corinthians
Galatians
Ephesians
Philippians
Colossians
1 Thessalonians
2 Thessalonians
1 Timothy
2 Timothy
Titus
Philemon

The General Epistles
Hebrews
James
1 Peter
2 Peter
1 John
2 John
3 John
Jude

Apocalypse
Revelation

Appendix B

BIBLE VERSES IN CHRONOLOGICAL ORDER

THE OLD TESTAMENT

Genesis 1, 2
Genesis 1:27
Genesis 3:1-5
Genesis 4:4
Genesis 5:24
Genesis 6:8-22, 7, 8, 9:1-16
Genesis 6:14
Genesis 12:1
Genesis 18:9-15
Genesis 27:27-40
Genesis 48:14-20
Genesis 50:25
Exodus 2:1-3
Exodus 3:14
Exodus 3:16-17
Exodus 20:1-17
Deuteronomy 7:9
Deuteronomy 31:6
Joshua 2:3-4
Joshua 24:14-15
Judges 6:11-12
Psalms 14:1
Psalms 16:11
Psalms 18:28-32
Psalms 32:5
Psalms 37:7
Psalms 103:1-4
Proverbs 1:7
Proverbs 3:5-6
Proverbs 4:19
Proverbs 6:16-19
Proverbs 11:18
Proverbs 22:17-19
Proverbs 27:17
Proverbs 27:20
Ecclesiastes 7:20
Ecclesiastes 12:13
Ecclesiastes 12:14
Isaiah 9:6
Isaiah 14:13-14
Isaiah 30:20
Isaiah 55:8-9
Jeremiah 29:11
Ezekiel 3:12
Daniel 4:34
Jonah 1:1-17

Appendix C

BIBLE VERSES IN CHRONOLOGICAL ORDER

THE NEW TESTAMENT

Matthew 2:1-11	Mark 14:10-26	John 10:17-18
Matthew 3:16-17	Mark 15:6-39	John 10:30
Matthew 4:1	Mark 16:1-19	John 11:40-44
Matthew 4:1-11	Luke 1:19	John 14:6
Matthew 5:1-2	Luke 2:7-17	John 14:16
Matthew 5:44	Luke 6:13-16	John 14:17
Matthew 6:6	Luke 6:46	John 14:26
Matthew 6:9-13	Luke 9:23-25	John 14:27
Matthew 6:19-21	Luke 9:58	John 15:7
Matthew 7:7	Luke 10:18	John 16:13-15
Matthew 7:13-14	Luke 11:1-4	John 19:1-36
Matthew 7:15	Luke 11:24-26	John 20:1-29
Matthew 7:21	Luke 11:28	Acts 1:9
Matthew 7:23	Luke 20:36	Acts 3:19
Matthew 10:2-4	Luke 22:3-23	Acts 5:1-11
Matthew 17:5	Luke 22:42	Acts 8:18-20
Matthew 18:21-22	Luke 23:1-47	Acts 8:30-31
Matthew 21:22	Luke 24:1-52	Acts 16:30-31
Matthew 22:34-40	John 1:1-5	Romans 1:20
Matthew 25:41	John 1:10	Romans 2:8-9
Matthew 26:14-30	John 1:14	Romans 3:17
Matthew 26:41	John 1:16	Romans 3:23
Matthew 27:1-54	John 2:7-11	Romans 8:5-6
Matthew 28:1-20	John 3:2	Romans 8:26-27
Matthew 28:16-20	John 3:6	Romans 10:9-10
Mark 3:16-19	John 3:16	Romans 12:2
Mark 6:38-44	John 3:19-21	Romans 12:19
Mark 10:45	John 6:35	Romans 14:11
Mark 11:23	John 8:12	Romans 15:4
Mark 11:24	John 8:44	Romans 16:17-18
Mark 11:25-26	John 10:9	1 Corinthians 9:25
Mark 13:22-23	John 10:10	1 Corinthians 15:3-4
Mark 13:31	John 10:14-15	

2 Corinthians 4:4
2 Corinthians 4:18
2 Corinthians 5:7
2 Corinthians 11:13
2 Corinthians 11:14
Galatians 3:22
Galatians 5:16-26
Galatians 5:19-23
Galatians 6:7
Ephesians 1:13-14
Ephesians 2:8-9
Ephesians 3:16
Ephesians 5:6
Ephesians 5:8-11
Ephesians 6:10-13
Ephesians 6:14-18
Philippians 2:4
Philippians 2:8
Philippians 2:14-15
Philippians 4:6
Philippians 4:7-9
Philippians 4:13
Philippians 4:19
Colossians 1:18
Colossians 2:6-7
Colossians 2:8
Colossians 3:13
Colossians 4:2
1 Thessalonians 2:19
1 Thessalonians 5:9
2 Thessalonians 3:16
1 Timothy 1:17
1 Timothy 4:6
1 Timothy 6:15
2 Timothy 2:15
2 Timothy 3:15
2 Timothy 3:16
2 Timothy 4:3-4
2 Timothy 4:8
Titus 3:4-5
Hebrews 1:14
Hebrews 4:16
Hebrews 11:1-39
James 1:2-5
James 1:12
James 1:13-15
James 1:19
James 4:2-3
James 4:7
1 Peter 4:11
1 Peter 5:4
1 Peter 5:6
1 Peter 5:8
2 Peter 1:20-21
2 Peter 2:1-3
2 Peter 2:4
1 John 1:5
1 John 1:7
1 John 2:15-16
1 John 3:23-24
1 John 4:1
1 John 4:7-13
1 John 4:9
1 John 5:10-12
1 John 5:14-15
1 John 5:19
Revelation 5:11
Revelation 12:7-8
Revelation 12:9
Revelation 20:11-15
Revelation 22:18-19

THE END

CPSIA information can be obtained
at www.ICGtesting.com
Printed in the USA
FFOW04n1753290316